Coloring book for adults and kids airplane image for design

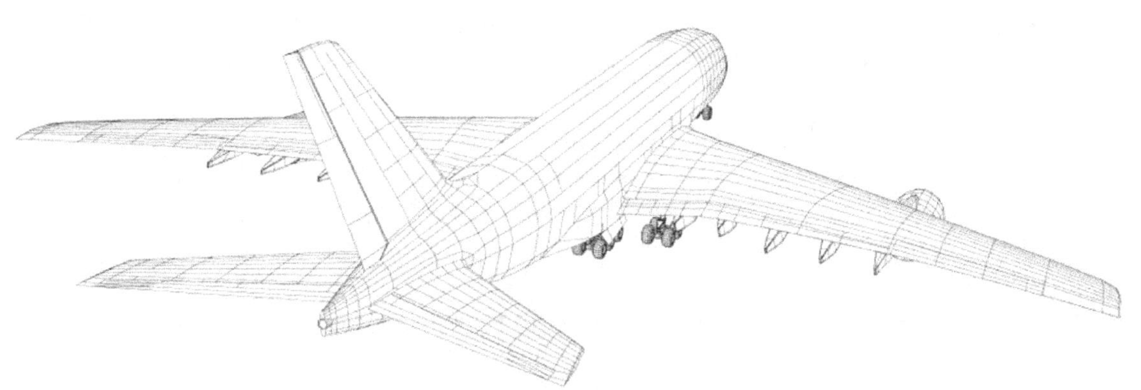

This coloring bookis belongs to

....

....

....

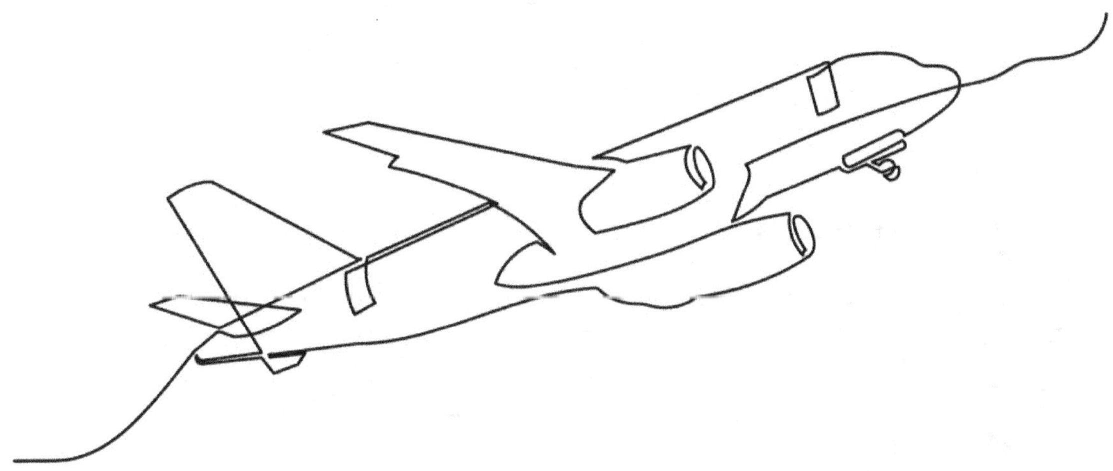

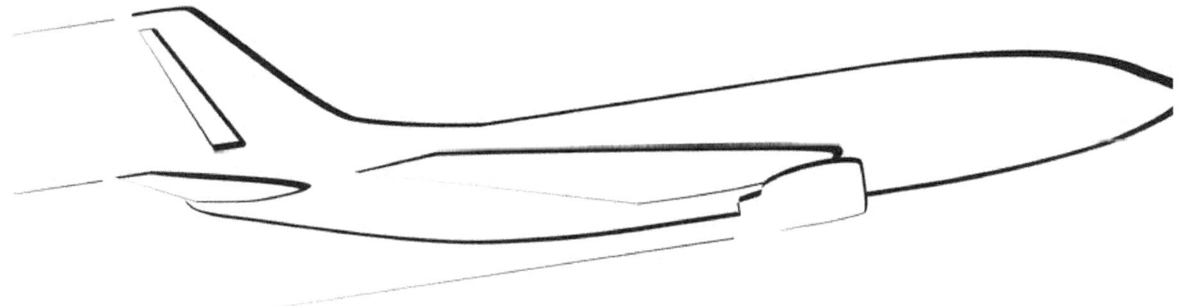

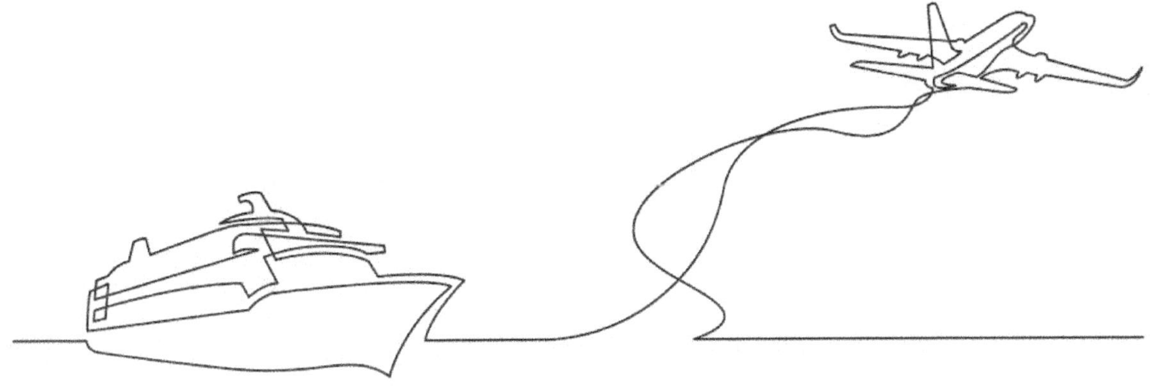

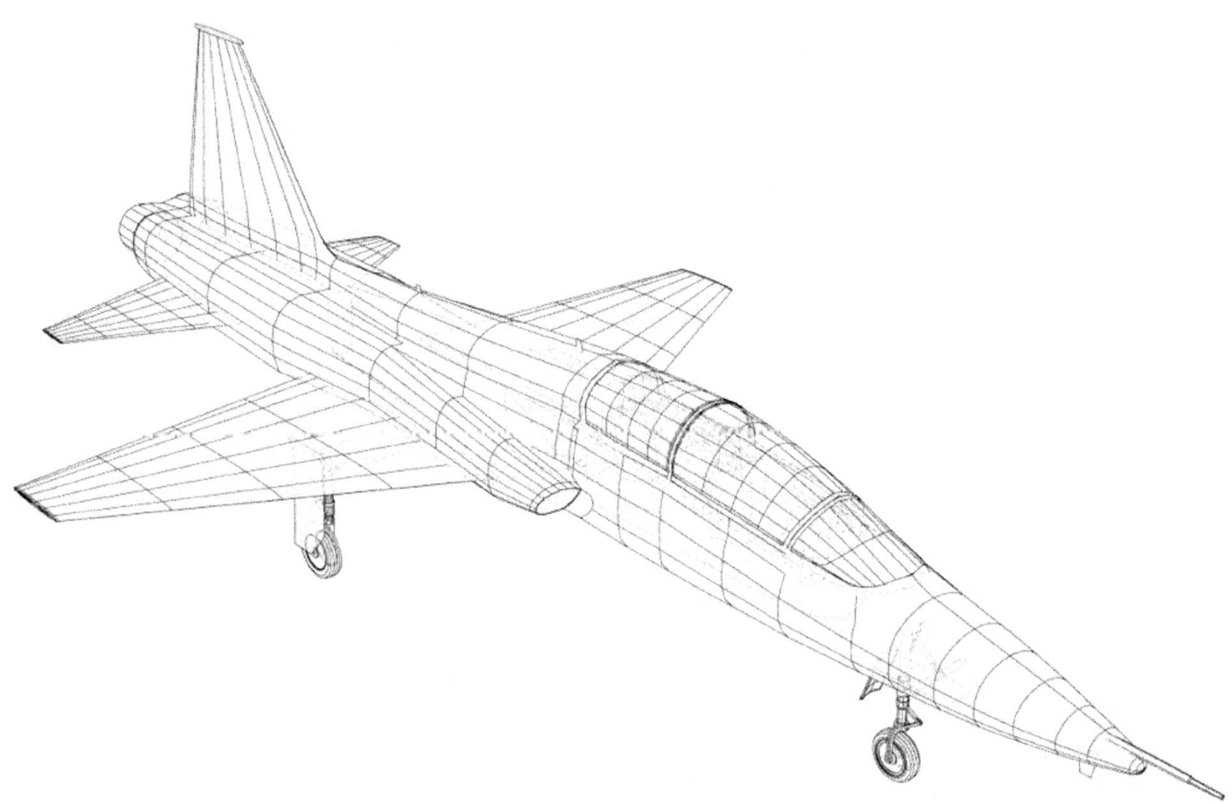

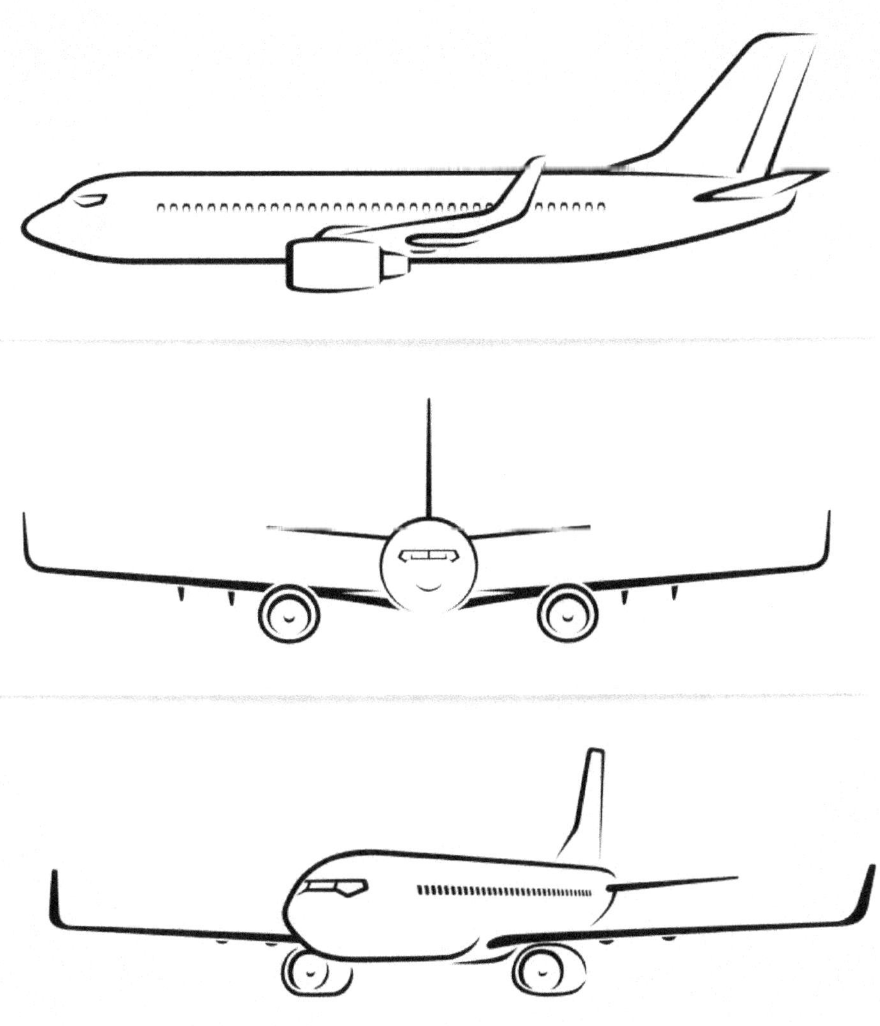

Let`s travel!

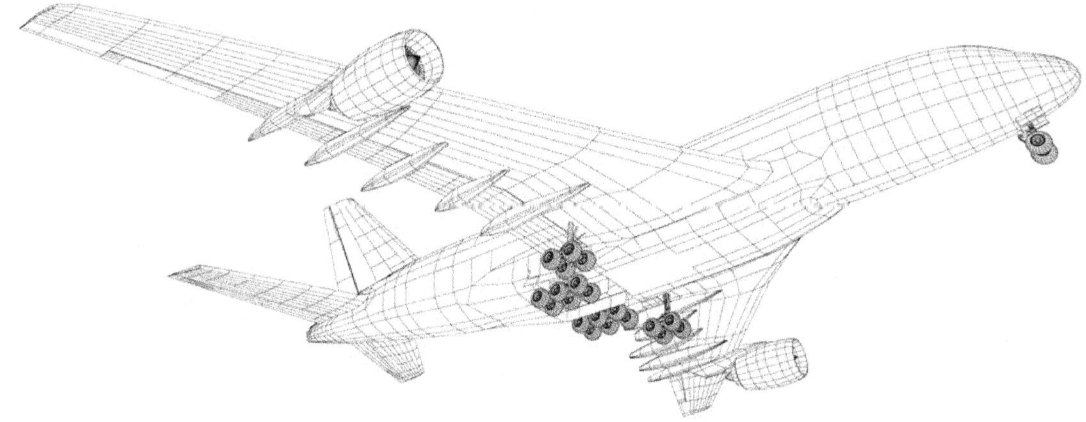

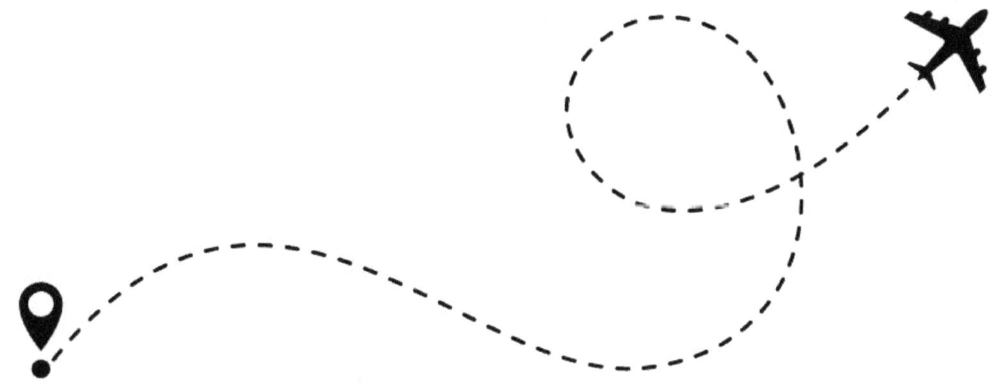

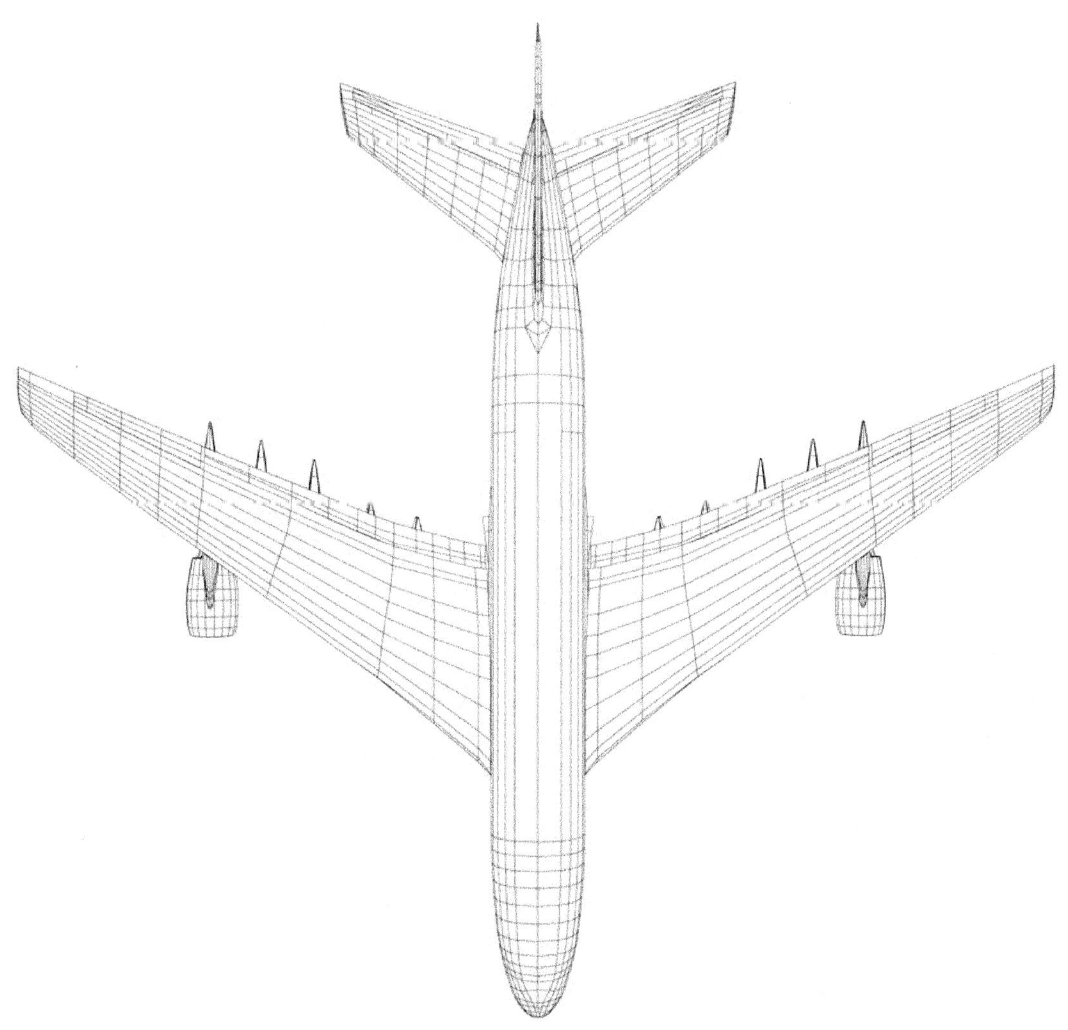

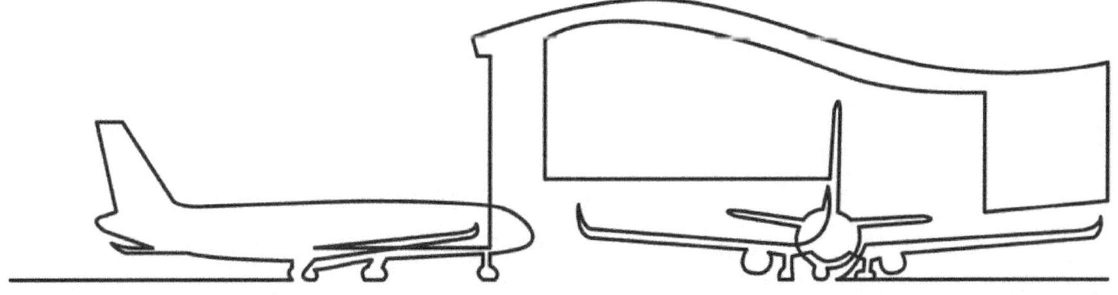

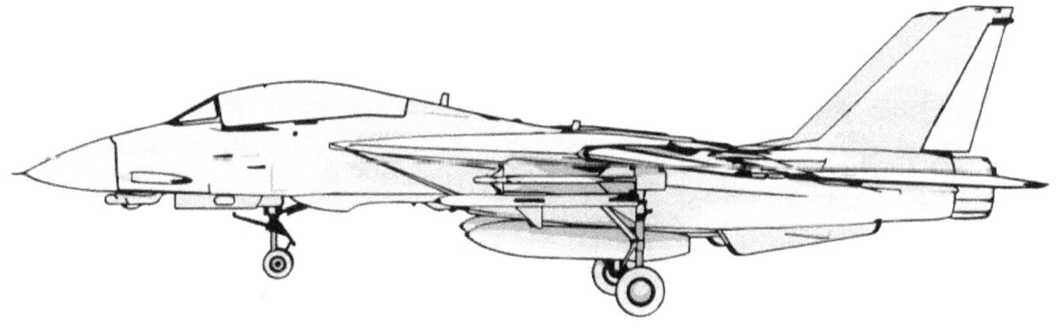

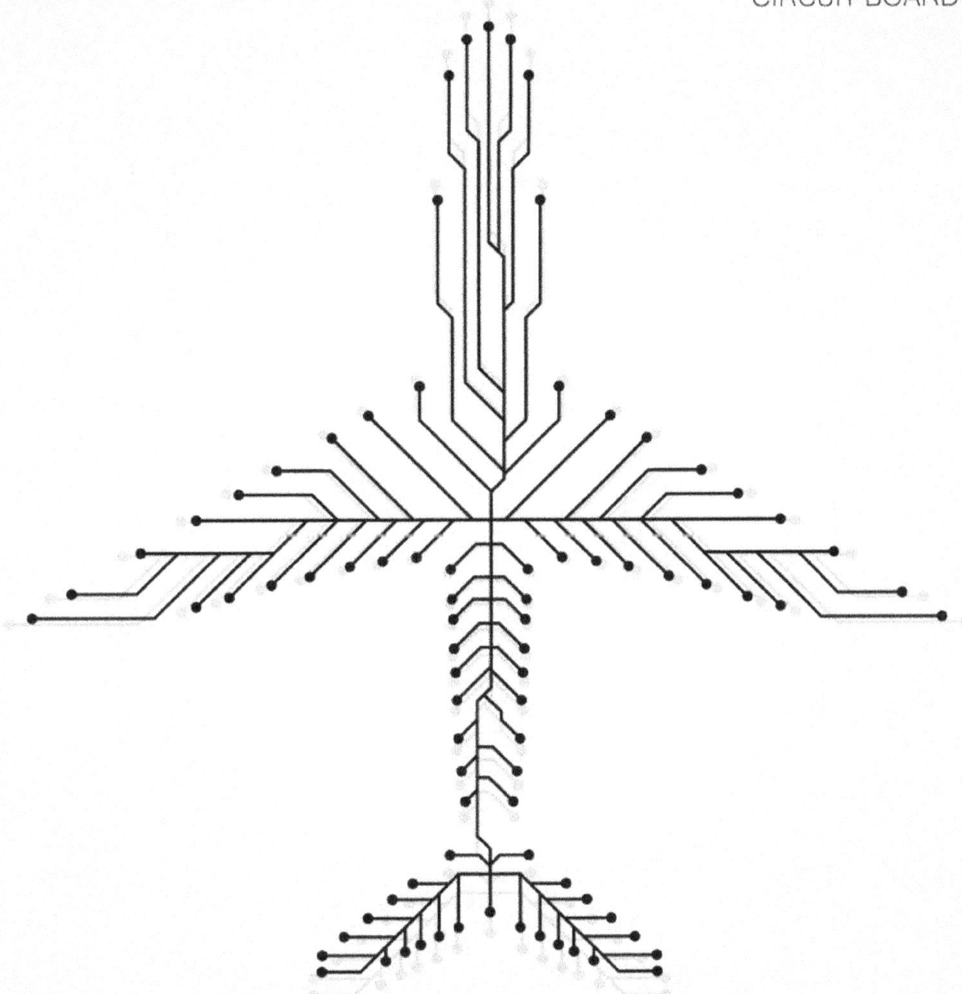

ABSTRACT AIRPLANE
CIRCUIT BOARD VECTOR

be happy

AIRPORT

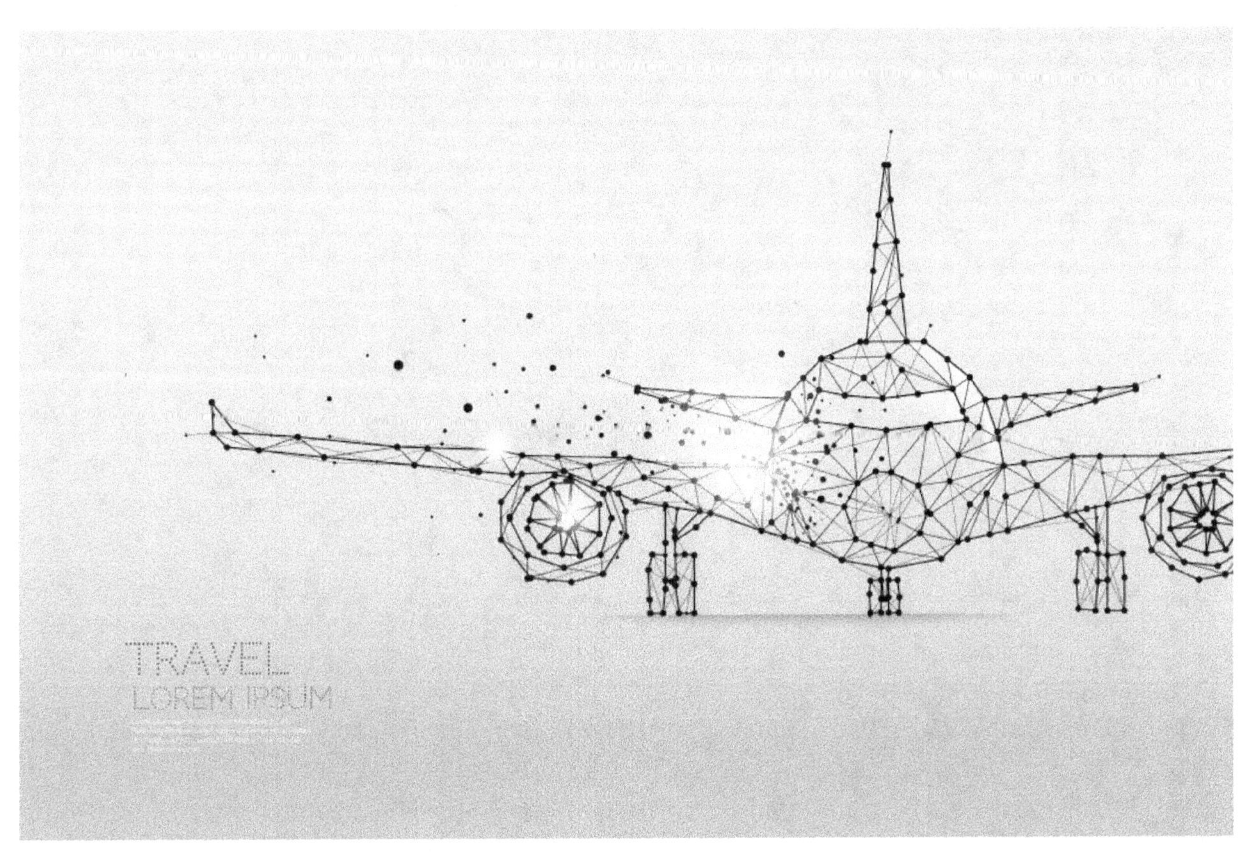
TRAVEL
LOREM IPSUM

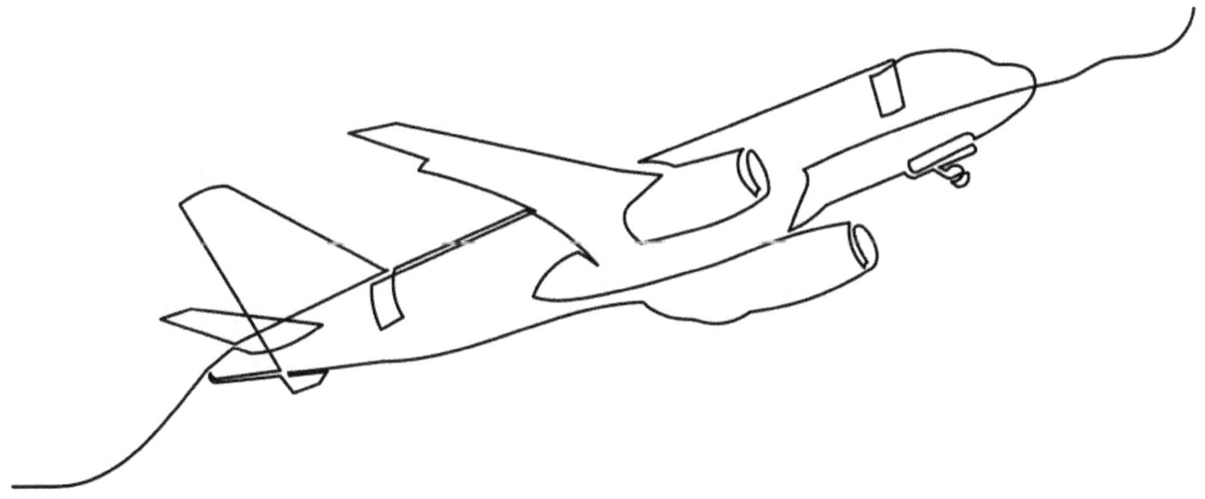

www.ingramcontent.com/pod-product-compliance
Lightning Source LLC
Chambersburg PA
CBHW080039260726
48658CB00007B/2665